O for a gun

101 haiku and senryu

Nigel Jenkins

Cover design and images by

David Pearl

Planet

First published
in Wales in 2007
by Planet

PO Box 44
Aberystwyth
Ceredigion SY23 3ZZ
Cymru/Wales

Printed by Gwasg Gomer
Llandysul, Ceredigion

The publisher acknowledges the financial support
of the Welsh Books Council

ISBN: 978-09540881-7-0

For Margot

ACKNOWLEDGEMENTS

Acknowledgements are due to the following publications in which some of these poems first appeared: *Planet*, *Roundyhouse*, and my 2006 collection *Hotel Gwales* (Gomer Press).
The cover image is of a 'Peacemaker' rifle, 1870's, USA, 'the gun that won the west'.

on their backs,

the two plastic chairs

in a swirl of leaves

how many of the dead,

as I climb these old stairs,

do I pass coming down?

my shadow at

sunset makes me

ten times the man

not crying

— this girl with hand to bowed head —

but phoning

only the blind man sees

that the leaf we're handing round

is a maple

over the rooftops

a white plastic bag breaks free

from the binmen

downpour —

smashed to steam

on slate roofs

the barmaid I once

craved — creased now, like me,

and double chinned

leaves blown up the hill

as gravity hurtles

my bicycle down

hooter booms —

and a slice of the city

sails into the night

leaves snowing

through the brazen blue,

and countable on trees

high tide, full moon and

fighter jets — if their pilots

could smell this woodsmoke

the seafront flags

winnowed, by autumn,

to ragged halves

a drink for old times —

afraid now even to touch

her arm

high tide after the storm,

the bay bobbing with

bits of forest

the reefer glows,

she exhales — across her smile

a cloud's shade

at dawn, as at dusk,

the windows of Swansea

take fire and burn

I open the window —

dogs barking in the nights

of childhood

no one about yet

except me and a rat —

who knows I'm trouble

'Real Morocco,' he gleams,

'hand-made

by the finest machines.'

no dog in sight …

but this man, for sure, is out

walking some hound

an orange —

the sun imagining

water

deluged at night,

the parked cars begin

to register alarm

'beware,' says the sign

at the churchyard gate,

'of unsafe gravestones'

the ashen light

at that window is not

tonight's moon

from the ice-rubbled

foreshore, twenty pale chunks

detach themselves and fly

the coos of a pigeon

loosening winter's iron —

snowdrops soon

it's boot to ball —

but a crow that comes sailing

up past my window

déja vu yawn —

but where exactly,

when?

a drop on my hand

from the bedside table — so,

the cracked glass leaks

last year's leaves —

a bushy oak rustling

in icy winds

an active hush ...

snow sensed even

before it's light ...

two men who never speak —

thrown together by ice,

their hats scattered

snow-grey skies ...

a chainsaw till dusk

echoes through the wood

colder, greyer …

the first ditherings

of snow

blizzard filling

sheep trods, rushing to plaster

the lengths of trees

kept awake —

by her sleepless

yawns

nothing, after snow,

for the nostrils — until the cobbler

opens his door

something, say the trees'

bony shadows, something is

about to happen

plough and tractor

mobbed by gulls; the sheen

of bladed earth

from beneath

the forgotten bramble pyre

a flaming of grass

but what I see

    as the jet whines in

    is the glide

of a gull

hot sun the day long

through leafless trees — summer

wearing spring's flowers

sunned earth fizzing

with rumours of barley

as the rain sinks home

solo cyclist —

shake, nod, shake of head — in deep

self-contention

windy demo —

swatted in the face

by a 'Peace' flag

'cancer ... ' she enquires,

noticing my weight loss,

'or a woman?'

a try! a try!

Cymru yes! could swing it yet —

the cats leave the room

eighteenth birthday

pre-party cloud

of aftershave and dope

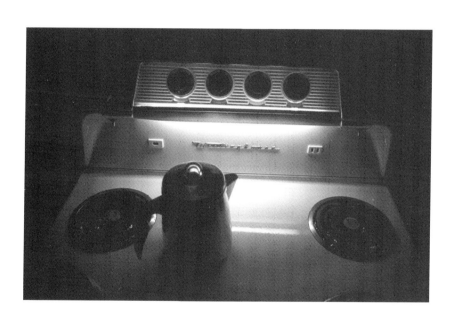

smoking fag-end

on the pavement — not a soul

to be seen

sun through mist

enkindling

the crows

cross-country nun

lost from sight in a field

of Friesians

the slaughterman halts,

opens a door to free himself

of a fly's buzz

a tree — an ash —

where once, I remember,

was none

puddle blocking path —

old enemies forced

to face each other

and now, with May,

after the south side blossoms

come those on the north

the sun's toil filling

east-facing rooms hours before

the workers arrive

the wind returns

— now the leaves are back with us —

in full voice

bend, blackbird,

where the phone wires ray,

o bend those notes

on the road to Hay,

a truck loaded with

white roses

Whit Monday high tide —

the jellyfish that happens

to be a balloon

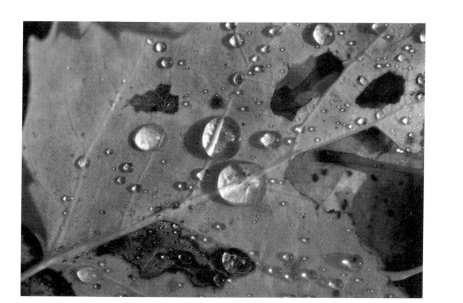

off-duty nurse,

mobile-rapt, smiling smugly

through the park

from the sunned hearse

June's heat blares

hill-top graves —

their headstones catching

the last of the light

city dog

delivered to the coast

barking at the sea

sky that seems blue;

this married man who

seems to be smiling

stop everything —

take careful note

of this hoppy belch

cyclist yawning

leaves in his wake

a trail of yawns

no rain all June —

the newspaper so much

noisier to turn

through the haze

across the bay — new-mown,

a field in the sky

she's been and gone:

on the black toilet seat,

a single red pube

worksheets across

the floor, making at night

paper moonshine

the ocean shredded

by jet-ski boymen …

the biding waves waving

first rain in weeks,

slugs risking freedom

on the busy path

the seal's head and mine

bobbing face to face

on the tide

no one, here,

stoops to the peach that lies

in the gutter

mighty gob-mouths

giggly with booze —

their baby-bottom heads

mobile in right hand,

she trades sweet nothings

as her left scoops poop

from nowhere, this hot

afternoon, a moan of wind,

the rattle of a can

caught, by some crone,

feasting my eyes on those

long brown legs

copper shafts

through bundling grey, beaming up

the Severn Sea

an escaped balloon

sails up past my window

pursued by wailing

cut-off jeans

— the sun less with us —

and a jumper too

a kiss — the last?

and I drive into the night

killing moths

clatterous thunder,

thunderous rain — drowning out

the foghorn

Committee Room 3,

window ajar, streams streaming

through the poplar leaves

though still some sun —

also, now, blackberries

and crickets

winos a-tiptoe

on midday streets, trying

not to wake us

half a dog-turd

bejewelled by a feasting

blowfly

leaf straining westward

— spider-anchored — when the treeful

roars east

my father's watch strap

still with scent, decades later,

of sour milk

have I learned?

since last I heard the buzzard's

day-long cry — nothing?

on the stairs at dawn,

deep inside the office block,

a single leaf

a mother's weary

smile, watching her son lob stones

into the sea

gull hooked, trailing

from its beak a yard of line —

o for a gun

barbie smoke, crickets —

and it's begun again

'to get late early'

sunlight sliding

down and up a spider's

invisible rope

the lipsticked wineglass —

re-filled, by sunrise, with

rainwater

though she's been gone

for months, they're still a couple

on the answerphone

the 'good morning' walker

greeting only

women

behind the dog man

a-swagger with leash —

a damp chihuahua

we do not see

til flight tilts them sunward —

oystercatchers

THE (SHORT) STORY OF THE HAIKU IN WALES:
AN AFTERWORD

Although haiku have been written in Wales since the 1960s, and it is possible to find proto-haiku in earlier manifestations of Welsh literary (and visual[1]) art, it is still early days for the haiku in this country. It may be the most popular form of poetry on the internet (a status not wholly to its advantage, given the deficiencies of many a net-borne 'haiku'), but the fact that most haiku written in Wales (in addition to related forms such as the senryu, the tanka and the haibun[2]) are published outside the country, chiefly in the specialist publications of England and the United States, suggests that this shortest of short poems is still some way from becoming an acceptable part of the Welsh literary scene. To admit, in 'mainstream' literary company, to an interest in the haiku is all too often to court withering scorn (leavened sometimes with pity) for the perceived futility of one's dalliance with such an alien and pointless fey trifle of a thing.

If the form remains much misunderstood, there are signs, nevertheless, that Wales's serious haiku practitioners, increasing in number from fewer than a dozen at the turn of the century to double that figure by 2007 — together with a larger number of 'mainstream' poets and creative writing students with an informed, if occasional, interest in the form — have between them contributed to making literary Wales rather more hospitable to the haiku than it used to be. Although the response, in a majority of cases, remains grudging, the doors of most Welsh journals are no longer automatically closed to the haiku poet, so that once in a while a tanka or two might tiptoe into the pages of *Planet* and a haibun might squeeze its way into *The New Welsh Review*; *Poetry Wales* may not be renowned as a haiku hotbed, but it is surely indicative of a welcome change in the literary climate that the one book that its editor, Robert Minhinnick, would take to the moon (according to an item in *The Western Mail*) is Robert Hass's splendid anthology *The Essential Haiku*[3]. Individual haiku and haibun collections from poets in Wales are multiplying — not all of them, these days, from haiku presses in England; by 2007, there were more than enough haikuists at work in Wales to justify the first ever Welsh anthology of haiku[4];

the British Haiku Society recently reported a significant increase in members from Wales; and practitioner critics such as Tony Conran and Ken Jones are beginning to lay down the critical foundations for the haiku's further development as a form adapting itself to Welsh conditions.

While it is true, as Robert Hass suggests, that 'What is in [haiku] can't be had elsewhere', the haiku — and haiku culture — are not as foreign to us as is sometimes assumed. The parallels between aspects of the early Welsh nature gnome and those of both the haiku and the tanka seem almost uncanny. Take, for instance, the thirty-six three-line (occasionally four-line) linked verses of *'Englynion Eiry Mynydd'* (lit. 'The stanzas of the mountain snow'; twelfth century, author(s) unknown), a selection of which appears in (unrhymed) translation in Tony Conran's *Penguin Book of Welsh Verse* (1967)[5] as 'Gnomic Stanzas'. Here are three of them:

Mountain snow, tossed by the wind;
Broad full moon, dockleaves green;
Rarely a knave's without litigation.

Mountain snow, stag in the ditch;
Bees are asleep and snug;
Thieves and a long night suit each other.

Mountain snow, bare tops of reeds;
Bent tips of branches, fish in the deep;
Where there's no learning, cannot be talent.

There are significant differences, of course, between the Welsh and the Japanese forms — the haiku's absence of regular rhyme, for instance; or the englyn's drive to conclusion, against the haiku's instinct to resist closure — but they have much in common. There's the three-line stanza (although a Japanese haiku traditionally appears as a single vertical line, it is divisible normally into three sections or phrases). There's the strict syllable count (7-7-7 syllables per line in this particular form of englyn, the *milwr*; 5-7-5 in a traditional, strict-form haiku[6]). There's the clear seasonal reference — the *kigo* that is characteristic of traditional Japanese haiku — and an almost scientific itemisation of natural phenomena, calling forth (in this case) the spirit of winter, ritualising knowledge of the seasons and reconciling people to their situation in the world and to the forces of nature that bear upon that world. There are the characteristic attributes of brevity, concision, simplicity, presence, sensory directness and present-tense immediacy. There's a quality of profound attention, often to minutiae, and a sharpness of observation mediated by down-to-earth, unembellished language[7]. While the first two lines of the Welsh tercet perform much like a haiku, the folksy sententiousness of the third line would seem to depart fundamentally from the haiku's refusal to pass comment. But the aphoristic conclusion drawn at the end of a Welsh gnomic stanza — sometimes rather obvious, but sometimes reminiscent of the oblique wisdom of an oriental koan — shares with many a tanka the moralising inclination of its last two lines. Although the haiku, developing away from the tanka and divesting itself of the older form's tendentious final lines, eschews judgemental generalisations, it is nevertheless profoundly interested, as is the Welsh nature gnome, in the conjunction of the human and the non-human.

Another striking parallel between the Welsh and the Japanese literary experience, at least in recent centuries, is an understanding of poetry as an egalitarian and communal activity, in which relatively large numbers of people from all sorts of social backgrounds participate, as both writers and informed readers. If the figure of about one million Japanese writing haiku today (out of a population of 128 million) would seem to give the Japanese a numerical edge over the Welsh in terms of popular engagement in poetry, the packed Eisteddfod pavilion on crowning and chairing days testifies to a broad-based and knowledgeable interest in poetry which is rare in Western countries. The englyn writer, like the haiku writer, engages with his or her form through a relationship with its past, the essence of which is transmitted by the teachings of an established practitioner and through face-to-face interaction with fellow poets. The notion of an apprenticeship is important in both cultures. What Mark Morris says about the Japanese creative context, in an essay on Buson (1716–84), strikes a notably Welsh chord: 'Shop owner, priest, samurai, actor, wealthy farmer, or petty bureaucrat, the poet was provided with a vantage point on the old poetry and a style growing from it contingent upon his teacher and his *haikai* ancestry. You belonged to all that and it to you ...'[8]

English theorists of the haiku such as R H Blyth (1898–1964), casting around for intimations of haiku sensibility in their own literary culture, have often lighted on the Romantic poets, Wordsworth above all, for inadvertent haiku moments, particularly in the poets' meditations upon landscape. With landscape looming so large in Welsh literature, it is no doubt possible to mine pre-modern Welsh poetry for accidental haiku snippets. The poetry of Dafydd ap Gwilym (*fl.* 1320–70), a Romantic (of sorts) centuries before 'The Romantics', might prove fruitful terrain for the haiku prospector.

In the trawling of these poetries for apparent resemblances, there lies of course the danger of overlooking significant differences and paying insufficient attention to the civilizational implications. What the poet of the nature gnomes is playing with, Tony Conran observes, 'is the recognition of patterns that have been vital to country people ever since the neolithic inventions of agriculture and livestock farming'; while the haiku developed as the art of a burgeoning, but initially despised and powerless, merchant class, disdainful of tradition and fixed on the moment:

The philosophies and life-styles behind the two kinds of verse are totally different. The englyn is rural, essentially a game based on countryside practical wisdom, which uses observation as an economic tool to survive; whereas the haiku is largely urban in origin, its raison-d'être not the directed trained eye of a farmer (say, looking for signs his crops are growing) but the bare awareness of meditation, taking in the 'inscape' of the scene before him as a way of Enlightenment...[9]

Real as the resemblances may be, they are no doubt largely accidental. For conscious and purposeful haiku activity in Wales, we have to look to the second half of the twentieth century — and to endeavours chiefly in the English language. The haiku, so far, has appealed to relatively few Welsh-language poets, preoccupied as many of them are with the masochistic pleasures of the formally more demanding englyn and other daunting structures. If all that most 'mainstream' poets 'know' of the haiku is that it calls for a 5-7-5 syllable count, it's small wonder that masters of the intricacies of *cynghanedd* are wont to dismiss the form as being too facile to be worthy of their attention — particularly if even the 5-7-5 'rule' has been abandoned by most contemporary English-language haikuists: all that's left, it must appear, is a smudge of directionless verbiage. There are other characteristics of the haiku that may not appeal to the exponent of (frequently ostentatious) Welsh word-craft: its innate humility; its plain-speaking lack of literary adornment; the almost complete absence of simile and the apparent paucity of metaphor (there *are* metaphors in haiku, but they are usually so undemonstrative as to be barely noticeable); the haiku's downplaying, therefore, of writerly skills (not to mention ego) and its foregrounding of the object and the moment of its attention. It is perhaps understandable that this seemingly fugitive form of open-ended minimalism — 'the poetry of emptiness', as it has been described, 'the half-said thing' — should have failed so far to make a significant mark in a nation of metaphor junkies, where the exuberant piling on of images, a practice known as *dyfalu*, has been such an admired feature of the *cywyddwr's* art.

Wales's first serious haiku poet, as far as I can see, is Tony Conran, who began writing haiku in about 1966 and whose enthusiasm for the form continues undiminished. In 2003, he published *Skimmings*, a collection of fifty-one haiku, and the haiku, 'as a kind of sketch-pad for ideas'[10], informs many of his non-haiku poems, such as the 'pastorals' in *Theatre of Flowers* (Gomer Press, 1998). At about the time that he was translating the poems that would appear in *The Penguin Book of Welsh Verse* — including, of course, those haiku-like gnomic stanzas — he was making his first foray into the realm of haiku by writing a renga[11] (it appears at the end of the radio ode 'Day Movements' in his *Poems 1951-67*). This, he admits, was not a 'proper' renga because, in the absence of informed collaborators, he wrote the whole thing himself. He was drawn to renga and haiku because

I wanted to escape from the English poetry market, which seemed to me (and often still does) to reduce poetry to a highbrow kind of I-it journalism, a dualism, that is, of the self which experiences and the world which is experienced. It is a dualism which dries up both self and world and bears very little relationship to the largely arbitrary it's and thou's which make up the flux of the moments where we actually live.[12]

Like any of the few in Britain at that time who were experimenting with haiku, he was working in complete isolation from others with a similar interest. Many of them may have felt, however — as he did — that the haiku answered a need of the time:

The sixties in general tried to cut themselves off from history except as a kind of flavour. The emphasis was on nowness, as in adverts or pin-ups. The haiku's isolation of the given moment as opposed to a continuous passage of constructed consciousness, as well as its minimalism (its 'slenderness'), had great appeal.[13]

A post-war enthusiasm in the United States for Japanese culture and religion had sparked a serious engagement with Zen aesthetics among the Beats, chief among them Jack Kerouac (1922–69), Allen Ginsberg (1926–97) and Gary Snyder (1930), the last two of whom were significant pioneers of the English-language haiku (although it should not be forgotten that an earlier generation had often fallen productively under the haiku's sway: William Carlos Williams (1883–1963) and Ezra Pound (1885–1972), for instance; and Wallace Stevens's (1879–1955) haiku-inflected 'Thirteen Ways of Looking at a Blackbird' would in time be echoed by Tony Conran's 'Thirteen Ways of Looking at a Hoover'). Although the haiku news from America was slow to arrive in Britain, there seemed by 1967 to be sufficient interest in the form for *The Guardian* to run a haiku competition: it attracted 3,000 entries, including some, interestingly, in Welsh.

The small-press scene in Britain, with its 'alternative' inclinations and built-in Zen enthusiasms, was considerably more receptive to the haiku (or what purported to be haiku) than most mainstream or 'establishment' outlets. Cardiff's Peter Finch, editor of the eclectic and influential magazine *second aeon* (1966–74), began writing haiku in the late 1960s, in addition to promoting the form in *second aeon* and in the No Walls readings and broadsheets; as a renowned concretist, he would later take the haiku into visual territory[14]. A prominent member of the London small-press scene in the 1960s was Edinburgh-born Chris Torrance who in 1970 moved to Wales, settling permanently at Pontneddfechan near Glynneath. As both haikuist and (crucially) teacher, Chris Torrance has played a vital and under-acknowledged role in helping to root the haiku in Welsh soil. If much of what passed for haiku in Britain until about 1990 was somewhat off the mark, Chris Torrance won international recognition as a genuine exponent of the art, publishing 'Seven Winter Haiku' in Mike Horovitz's famous Penguin anthology *Children of Albion: Poetry of the Underground in Britain* (1969) and being hailed in America, in William J Higginson's landmark 'how to' guide, *The Haiku Handbook* (1985), as one of the four most significant haiku poets of Britain. His pioneering extra-mural creative writing classes at the University of Wales, Cardiff (now Cardiff University) — which were eventually strangled by bureaucracy in the 1990s — introduced scores of venturesome new writers to the haiku and its related forms.

The 1970 to 1990 period in Wales, as in Britain generally, seemed to generate little haiku activity, with mainstream poets tending to dismiss the haiku as some faddy hangover from the 1960s — if, indeed, they paid it any regard at all. But quietly, haphazardly, some sort of foundation was being laid. Tony Conran in the north was persevering with his one-man renga-making (see, for example, 'Ten Morning Songs' in *Spirit Level*, Gomer, 1974) and experimenting with tanka ('Six Poems about God', in the same volume). Peter Finch and Chris Torrance in Cardiff, and Phil Maillard and I in Swansea were offering the haiku as an essential component of writing courses for organisations such as the Welsh Academy, the WEA and university extra-mural departments, and there was occasional contact with established haikuists from further afield. Bill Wyatt, for instance, another 'Child of Albion' and one of the few English haiku writers at that time to have been noted in America, gave a memorable reading in the early 1980s — of nothing but haiku —to a capacity audience in Swansea's Singleton Hotel.

Since about 1990, the haiku pace has perceptibly quickened. The founding in that year of the

British Haiku Society — by the English haikuists David Cobb and Dee Evetts — gave haiku enthusiasts their first opportunity to meet each other, and to debate, publish and promote a literary form whose development in the countries of Britain had been impeded by the isolation of its practitioners and by the lack of consensus as to what, in British and European terms (rather than according to the dominant American view), might constitute a functioning haiku on this side of the Atlantic. Respecting the integrity of the nations and regions of Britain, the BHS has sought to foster not 'the British haiku' (perish the grotesque thought) but a theory and practice appropriate to the making of haiku wherever in these islands poets find themselves working. Although some sort of definitional consensus — which pays proper regard to Japanese essentials while acknowledging the need to adapt the form to indigenous conditions — seems by now to have been reached, vigorous debate continues on many related issues, with national and regional branches flying the flag for local particularity and diversity. Perhaps only half of Britain's haiku writers belong to the BHS, but all have benefited from its educational and promotional work and from the articulate advocacy of local representatives such as Ken Jones in Wales, who has sought to understand and develop the haiku in Welsh cultural terms.

The first event of national significance in the development of the haiku in Wales was the Welsh Academy's 1991 Japan Festival Haiku Competition, which was the first major international haiku contest to be organised in any of the countries of Britain for twenty-four years. It attracted over a thousand entries in English from all over the world, although only three of the Welsh entries — one by Marc Evans of Cardiff, and two by John Rowlands of Cardiff, writing out of experimental choice not in his mother tongue, Welsh, but in English — made it through to the 'highly commended' category. Part of the prize was publication in *The New Welsh Review*[15]. As co-judge (with David Kerrigan), I wrote an introductory article to the selection, pointing out that 'In publishing the three prize-winning poems and twenty of the highly commended, the *NWR* is the first Welsh magazine in decades to pay serious attention to this popular but frequently misunderstood form.' In fact, with the exception of *second aeon*, it was probably the first Welsh magazine ever to pay the haiku attention of any kind.

The winner of that competition was David Cobb who by then was well on his way to becoming one of the most accomplished haikuists in the English-speaking world[16]. He has maintained contact with the developing haiku scene in Wales ever since. In 1992, Garden Festival Wales at Ebbw Vale employed him as resident haiku poet for the festival's oriental week, and more recently he has visited Swansea on a couple of occasions to take part in various haiku events at the Dylan Thomas Centre and the university. On one such occasion, five of Wales's haiku poets — Ken Jones, Noragh Jones, Peter Finch, Arwyn Evans and I combined with musicians Peter Stacey and Dylan Fowler to present an innovatory programme of haiku backed by minimalist improvisations on flute and guitar.

A more significant innovation in Wales (as in England) since about the late 1990s has been the haibun, an appealing fusion of haiku and haiku-like prose which was once widespread in Japan — Bashō's seventeenth-century classic *The Narrow Road to the Deep North* being the most famous example of the genre — but which has been virtually dormant there for a century or more. While David Cobb, initially, led the way in England, the pioneers in Wales have been Ken Jones, Noragh Jones and Matt Morden. The publication in 2001 by Ken Jones's Pilgrim Press of a three-man[17] haiku and haibun anthology, *Pilgrim Foxes*, was a milestone. The English haiku and haibun poet George Marsh wrote in his introduction: 'This book will be a collectors' special: it contains the first mature masterpieces in a new Western literary genre, the haibun ... As you read you see all three [poets] making discoveries which will become important to all of us in the literature of the unfolding century.'

As well as publishing haiku and haibun, Ken Jones has also been concerned to disseminate his thoughts on the theory of these forms, particularly as there is not yet the consensus about the nature of the haibun as there is about that of the haiku. Another significant Welsh theorist of the haiku is Tony Conran, most of whose invaluable insights on this subject have been confined so far to personal communication in letter form. His elucidation of the three classical attributes of the haiku is worth quoting at length:

The haiku is a sociable but not a social form. It is almost totally unrhetorical, having nothing to say to the will. It does not have an agenda of social change, except possibly to persuade other people to write haiku in reply. From all this flow the three classical haiku attributes — loneliness, tenderness and slenderness. A haiku represents a sharing of a moment in a great loneliness; what is shared is centred on the feeling of loneliness itself, however much other feelings are involved with it. Loneliness is the gift the haiku poet prizes above all, because it is the loneliness of detachment, not the bitter isolation of frustrated desire. Within that detachment one's feelings can grow, not as the ravishers of virtue they normally are, but as Christ says God feels compassion for the fall of a sparrow. Haiku poets like Bashō call it tenderness — fellow-feeling, a gentle acknowledgement that things exist outside yourself, which suffer and have their being in the Tao of enlightenment just as you do. And a haiku must be slender because it makes no claims upon you other than an invitation to share its moment.[18]

Like Ken Jones, he acknowledges the importance of a shared understanding of what the haiku is about. Some informal renga experiments with friends might have got somewhere had there been poets to call upon who knew what they were doing:

If all the poets of Wales could be given prison-sentences — say, six months — and told they had to split into groups of five and each group to produce at least 20 haiku a day, gradually increasing to 100, we might find ourselves in a tradition where haiku-writing was the norm, and, more important, had standards and a literary aesthetic of its own.[19]

Over the last decade or so, the universities have played an increasingly significant role in establishing a haiku aesthetic. In 2001, Martin Lucas, studying at Cardiff, completed his groundbreaking PhD thesis, *Haiku in Britain, Theory, Practice, Context*, and the creative writing faculties of most of Wales's higher education establishments have at least one member of staff who is experienced in and enthusiastic about the haiku, from Carol Rumens at Bangor to Philip Gross at Glamorgan. (On the other hand, unlike in England, there is no statutory obligation to teach the haiku in Welsh schools; although teachers are free to introduce the form if they wish, one suspects that in most cases consideration of the haiku advances little beyond the counting of syllables.)

As the debate broadens and matures, and as more haiku and haibun are published here, there are encouraging signs that a haiku aesthetic pertinent to Welsh cultural conditions is beginning to be articulated (although it has to be said that by no means all of Wales's haiku writers conceive of themselves as operating in a Welsh literary context). As elsewhere, the haiku has its dedicated specialists who tend to devote most of their energies to that form and its relations, chief among them Ken Jones (whose haiku are informed by, and a function of, his Zen Buddhism), Noragh Jones (who sometimes writes in Welsh), Matt Morden, Arwyn Evans, Jane Whittle and Caroline Gourlay (editor, from 1998 to 2000, of the BHS journal *Blithe Spirit*). But there are increasing numbers of 'mainstream' poets, in or of Wales, for whom the haiku constitutes an important part of their poetic endeavour, among them Tony Conran, Chris

Torrance, Peter Finch, Carol Rumens, Philip Gross, Lynne Rees and Humberto Gatica, who writes in Spanish. The perceived divide between the two apparent 'communities' — with the haiku specialists sometimes complaining that too many mainstream poets' haiku are distractingly 'literary', if not verging on 'poesy', and the mainstream establishment declining to recognise the specialists as 'serious' poets (and publishable, therefore, in mainstream outlets) — has tended to retard the haiku's development (on both sides of the Dyke). So too has the fact that until recently few of Wales's serious haiku practitioners have been under fifty years of age. In the last few years, however, several promising young poets with a more occasional but nevertheless knowledgeable commitment to the form have begun to emerge from the growing number of creative writing classes. The haiku may have some distance to travel before it can be said to have 'arrived' in Wales, but it seems, at last, to be on the way.

1. In the afterword to my earlier haiku collection, *Blue* (Planet Books, 2002), I suggested that the painter Thomas Jones, Pencerrig (1742-1803) — unaware as he would almost certainly have been of this Japanese tradition — had accorded 'revolutionary and haiku-like attention' to the crumbling backstreets of Naples in, for example, his now famous 16cm by 11cm study 'A Wall in Naples' (1782).
2. Senryu: a form of haiku that foregrounds humour. Tanka: a five-line poem, predating the haiku, that tends to focus on love and nature. Haibun: a fusion of haiku and haiku-like prose, little practised in Japan since the end of the nineteenth century, but attracting increasing numbers of haiku poets in Britain and North America.
3. Robert Hass (ed.), *The Essential Haiku: Versions of Bashō, Buson, and Issa* (Ecco, New York, 1994).
4. This anthology, edited by Arwyn Evans, is due to be published by Gwasg Carreg Gwalch sometime in 2007.
5. Subsequently re-issued by Seren Books, in a new edition, as *Welsh Verse* (1986).
6. Since about 1900 in Japan, and more recently in North America and Britain, there has developed a growing acceptance of the 'free form' haiku in which the 17-syllable 'rule' is often relaxed, so that haiku may occasionally have more than 17 syllables, but usually aim to have fewer: sufficiency is the goal. Some practitioners prefer a pattern of stresses (2-3-2) as a more amenable approximate template than a 5-7-5 syllable count.
7. Some of these shared attributes, Tony Conran suggests in a letter to me dated 20.12.06, 'may have something to do with the oceanic and changeable weather of both Britain and Japan, both of them archipelagos offshore of continental land-masses, both of them producing exceptionally innovative gardeners ...'

8. Mark Morris, 'Buson and Shiki: Part One', *Harvard Journal of Asiatic Studies* 44, No.1.

9. From Tony Conran's letter of 20.12.06.

10. From a letter to me from Tony Conran dated 29.9.2003.

11. Renga: a chain of linked haiku, normally produced collaboratively.

12. From Tony Conran's unpublished essay 'Haiku as an English poetic form: a personal approach'.

13. Ibid.

14. See his collection *The Welsh Poems* (Shearsman, 2006).

15. *The New Welsh Review* No. 15 (Vol. IV, No. 3; Winter 1991-92).

16. For a profile of David Cobb, see my essay 'Batting for Essex, England — and the World' in *Planet* 173, October/November 2005.

17. The three *Pilgrim Foxes* are Ken Jones and two Irish poets, James Norton and Seán O'Connor.

18. From Tony Conran's letter of 29.9.2003.

19. Ibid.

I am grateful to David Cobb, Tony Conran, Arwyn Evans, Peter Finch and Ken Jones for reading an earlier draft of this afterword and for making valuable suggestions for its improvement. Any remaining errors of fact or judgement are mine.